luna osho

echoes
of the heart

illustrated by the author

**a poetry collection on
love and loss**

copyright © 2023 by luna osho

all rights reserved. no part of this book may be used or reproduced in any manner whatsoever without written permission except in the case of reprints in the context of reviews.

first edition - june 2023

cover design: luna osho

ISBN: 979-8783461613

for my love
my life
my everything

contents

acknowledgment	8
blossoming love	11
intertwined souls	29
fragments of loss	47
resilient hearts	65
eternal echoes	83
about the author	100

acknowledgment

i would like to express my deepest gratitude to all those who have supported me in bringing to life, "echoes of the heart". though i prefer to remain anonymous, your unwavering encouragement and love have made this journey possible.

first of all, i am grateful for the profound complexities of love and loss, which are the essence of this collection. they have whispered their truths to me, guided my pen, and painted the canvas of my words.

to my readers, known and unknown, your unwavering support and open hearts have given wings to my verse. your acceptance of vulnerability and your willingness to embark on this poetic journey fills me with immeasurable joy.

thank you to everyone closest to me for your faith in my voice and unwavering encouragement. your presence has been the beacon that has lit my path, even in the darkest nights of doubt.

finally, to the mysterious moon, luna osho, who finds solace in anonymity, thank you. for your endless inspiration, for allowing me to plunge into the depths of my soul, and for being a guiding light in this enigmatic exploration of the heart.

may "echoes of the heart" resonate within you, dear reader, and may its words take you on a beautiful journey where love and loss dance together as eternal partners in our human existence.

with the deepest gratitude,
luna osho

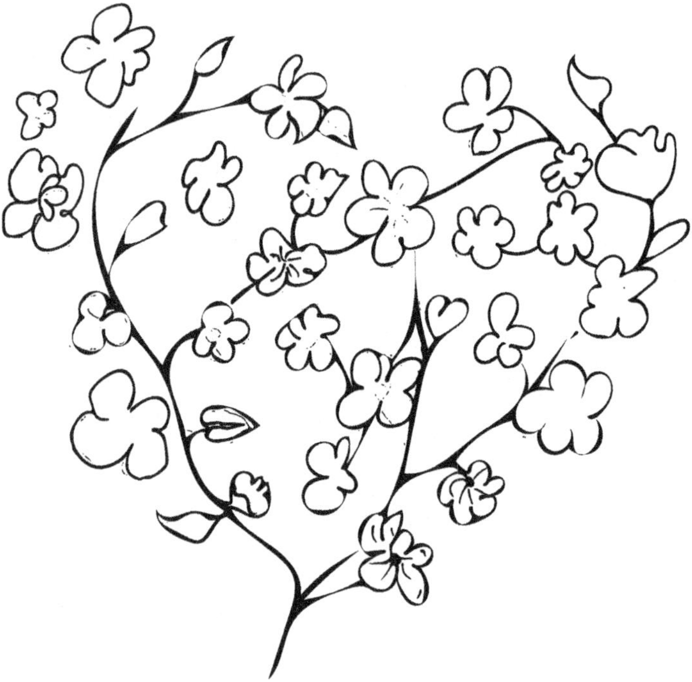

blossoming love

the first time

i saw you

it was like a flower

opening up

for the first time

in a field of

newborn sunflowers

i saw your face

like a door opening

to an unfamiliar room

and suddenly

the void within me

did not feel so big

anymore

i have always felt

that love at first sight

is nothing but a fantasy

until now

when one is in love

butterflies flutter around

a tingling sensation

like fireworks

that want to burst

out of the body

how long will it take
before we will hold hands
and gaze into each other's eyes
for the very first time

how long will we wait
before we let our walls down
and let ourselves fall in love
with someone new

i'm waiting for him

to come home

to me

i think i love you
the words bubble up from my heart
surging forth from my soul
my eyes meet yours
and i am lost in them forever

i want to hold your hand
to touch your soft skin
to caress your cheeks

your smile illuminates the night
like the moon
your eyes like stars
they shine so bright

how can i not fall in love?
i know now it was always you
always

there is no such thing

as perfect relationships

no one knows

how it will turn out

take your chances

let yourself feel

what you feel

today

how long will we wait

to find love

and live our lives

together

how long before we hold hands

and dance under the stars

in the night air

with music and laughter

singing in our hearts

how long before we stand under the moon

and look up at the stars

in awe at the beauty above

to dream of the magic to come

how long before we share our hearts

and lay bare the secrets of our souls

how long before we finally know

the things that can't be named

how long to reach the stars

or plumb the depths of the sea

and touch the edge of eternity

i'm glad you took my hand

i'm glad i took your hand

i'm glad we took each other's hand

together

in this journey

through this fairy merry land

you are a gift

from heaven

my forever treasure

we are a song

with each its own melody

sung together

in a harmony that is only ours

a duet

a duet of love

we are like a dance

with each its own part

danced together

in a pas de deux that is only ours

a tango

a tango for two

i fell in love with you the first time i saw you

you were like a ray of sunshine

and i knew i would never see someone like you again

i had to get to know you

i had to find out what your favorite food was

your favorite movie

how you spent your summers as a child

how you felt about kids

how you liked to spend your weekends

what made you laugh

what made you cry

what made you smile

what made you mad

i wanted to know everything about you

and i still do

we found our home
our love
our everything

we found each other
and our home is not a place
it is a feeling
an emotion
and it is love

we will grow old
we will grow strong
we will grow together

always

you are the first thought in my head

and the last thought on my mind

you are within me

all the time

i don't think i can ever find love like this again

and even if i could

i only want to be with you

forever

i fell in love with love
and thought love was

i fell in love with love
but learned it isn't simple

love is messy and complicated
love is hard work and not always kind
it isn't always as gentle as imagined
there are no guarantees

and that's what i love about love
it's never predictable
always a surprise

i fell in love with love
and i'll fall in love again

i believe in love
i believe in you

our love is timeless

our love will never die

it will grow and be bright

it will last forever

like the stars

like the moon

like you

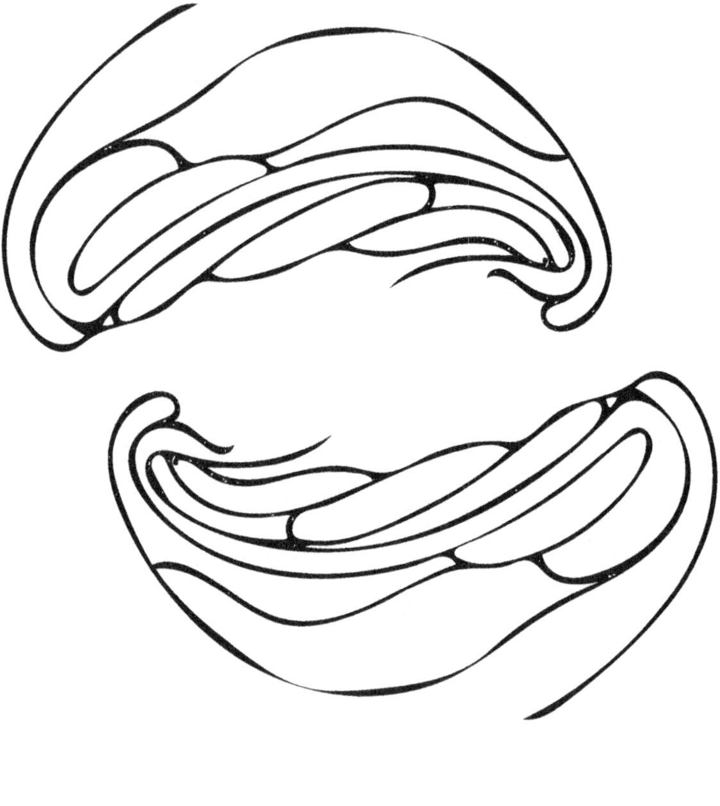

intertwined souls

you bring me

light

in the darkness

like the moon

when everything else is gone

you are my sun

when the clouds have covered the sky

you are my warmth

when all is lost

you are my way home

when i am far away

you are the one i love

the one i call mine

you are the light that guides me

through this dark world

the stars above us glow

like the fire that dances

within my heart

as you whisper sweet nothings

into my ears

you light up my life

with your magic smile

your eyes shine bright

and your laugh fills the starry night

you are my moon

my sun

and my sky

echoes of the heart

my love

i have one request

stay with me

don't go

let me be with you

forever

you complete me
like no one else can
and my life is bright
when you are at my side

our souls are intertwined

and we belong together

like two pieces of the same puzzle

no matter how far apart

we'll always find each other

we'll always come back

to our true home

and our true love

there are a thousand ways to love you
and a thousand ways for me to show it
whether by holding your hand
or just listening when you speak

there are a million ways to love you
and a million ways for me to show it
whether by kissing your lips
or just watching you sleep

there are infinite ways to love you
and i will do my utmost to show them all

we are woven together in time
like a harp's strings
waving its ethereal harmony
into the ultimate melody

the breath of our lives
mingle our hearts
in love and passion

we are bound together
by a chain so strong
that even a pause
will not be able
to silence our melody

you are the air
without i can not
live

i could spend a lifetime writing about you
and it wouldn't be enough
i could write a thousand books
and it still wouldn't be enough
i could paint you a thousand pictures
and still it wouldn't be enough

you are the well
from which i draw my inspiration
you are the air
that gives me new energy
you are the warmth
that eases my heart

when i am with you
i leave the world behind
to join the stars in the sky
and sail the waves
to a place where only we exist

our own little paradise

you are the wave

that calms my soul

you are the flower

that blossoms my heart

you are the wind

that sweeps my thoughts

you are the love

that fills my spirit

you are the happiness

i have always longed for

your eyes embrace

a thousand stories
i wish i could live

a thousand songs
i wish i could hear

a thousand poems
i wish i could read

what we have

is a miracle

it's a mystery

a tale that never ends

it's everything and nothing

it's you and me

my heart aches
as it yearns for you to be near

i could stare at your eyes for a lifetime
and still not know everything about you

i could write a book
and still
not be able to tell
every single story you've ever been through

i could spend a lifetime and still not find
the words to define you

how long until he realizes

i am not what he wants

how long until i realize

he is not what i want

fragments of loss

i wish you were here
with me
sitting by my side
in this night
when all is quiet
and all is still

you're not here
and my heart is breaking
i look into the stars
and i think of you
and i wonder
why can i not be with you

i miss you

we were in love

but you were taken from me

in an instant

how could you just leave me?

why didn't you say goodbye?

you promised me forever

and now it's over

please come back

please, come back

to me

i see you everywhere
in my thoughts
in the eyes of everyone
in my dreams

but you're never there
you are gone
and all that remains is a phantom
that haunts me day and night

you're not here
and loneliness eats
my soul from within

i need you
my heart screams
in silence

i'm lost

i wish we could have

been together

until the stars burn out

and the earth goes dark

until there is nothing left

but ashes and dust

when you left me with nothing but a kiss
and the scent of your skin on my lips
i felt as if my world collapsed
and was filled with darkness

when i opened my eyes and saw
nothing but shadows in my room
i thought i could never be happy again
nor would i know love

echoes of the heart

i remember

the way you

used to kiss my forehead

how you would whisper

words of love

into my heart

the pain of your loss
is still sharp
like a knife
cutting deep
inside my heart

i feel your loss
every night
in every moment
of every day

i feel you
with me
your absence
like a black hole
consuming me

without words
i knew you loved another
we didn't talk about it
and i hoped for you to say
anything

i waited
and waited
but you never said a word

and now you're gone
and i don't know how to live
with the wound it made

i know you've come home late before
but it's different today

i long for your footsteps
i listen
and listen still

no sound comes from the stairs

and when the morning is there
i wake up in the silence of an empty room
with only cracks in my heart

and it hits me
hard

when people ask how
i cope with my loss
my words feel heavy
and i feel how they crash
on their way out

what can i possibly say
that could do justice to what i feel
the pain is there
and nothing
will make it stop

sometimes, i wish i could rewind time

so we could have another chance

to do everything over again

and maybe this time

it would work

when i think about you
i feel my chest squeeze
like it's been held in a grip
with no escape

and i feel small
and insignificant
like a grain of sand
in the vast expanse of the universe

i wonder
would anyone miss me
if i were to disappear
would someone care
or would someone cry
would someone scream
or would someone notice

i'm here

there was a time when you loved me

you held me in your arms

and you kissed me on the forehead

and you told me how much you cared

and you promised me a lifetime together

and you asked me to marry you

and i said yes

and we walked into the sunset

holding hands

and i believed in the promise of forever

how do you get over someone
when you still love him
desperately

i know you're gone
but i can't stop thinking about you
you're always in my head
even though you're not
and i still can't believe it happened

i never thought it would be like this
i thought we would grow old together
and that we'd die together
in our sleep

and finally succumb into
eternity

i loved your eyes

they were bright

full of hope

like a sunrise in my sight

full of promise

i loved your laugh

they were sweet

full of passion

like music to my ears

full of joy

i will never have the chance to see or hear them again

i see you everywhere

where the sun rises

and the birds sing

where the seasons change

where the moon is full

and the stars shine

you are always there

you are the melody

and the rhythm

that guides me

in life

resilient hearts

after you left me

i felt disoriented

as if i woke up from a dream

i was unsure of my future

i took a deep breath

and tried to find my way

through a world without you

then i understood

it wasn't just a dream

that i just woke up

into a new reality

i have to let go

move on

and try again

i am not

broken

i am only

mending

we only want to heal

but sometimes it takes

time and patience

to get there

and that's okay

there are days

that i wake up

in tears

remembering

you are gone

but others

i'm not sad

because i know

there are other people

who are just as lonely

the fear of the unknown
makes me tremble in my boots
while hiding in the hills

it keeps me up at night
makes me doubt my every move
i don't think
i'm ready
for whatever might come

but i suppose it's okay
no one else
is either

i wish you had told me
about the dark
before it came

i would have prepared for it
so i would have been ready
for the battle that layed ahead

luna osho

tomorrow is the beginning
of a new day
the first step toward the future
as the journey of love goes on

no matter how many times we get lost
we have to start over
it may not always turn out right
but there's always room to learn
and to grow

i feel alive today

as i look back

at the thought

that your departure would be

the end of my world

now i see

how i was wrong

the road ahead is

a little bumpy

but i am not scared

my love is here

with me

echoes of the heart

i'm still trying

to get better

and as my heart

gets stronger day by day

my wounds

are mend with gold

thus leaving only scars

as proof of the battles

i fought

and won

i'm okay now

no need to try

just do

feel

and love

i spent so much time

worrying

about the past

or the future

for nothing

echoes of the heart

once i didn't believe

another could love me

now i know

if a girl can love herself

only then

another can love her

i want to believe

in happy endings

and fairytale love

soulmates

i want to believe

there is a storyboard

where everything works out

where there is a person

who loves me

for who i am

so many things

i haven't done yet

and so many things

i've yet to discover

but the world is too big

for me to grasp

on my own

even though it may hurt sometimes

loneliness can be overcome

let us not give up

as we strive for happiness

a new love

and another star to guide our way

my feelings

have always been there

unspoken

shrouded in doubt

but now

i am free to feel

to express

to live

to be

eternal echoes

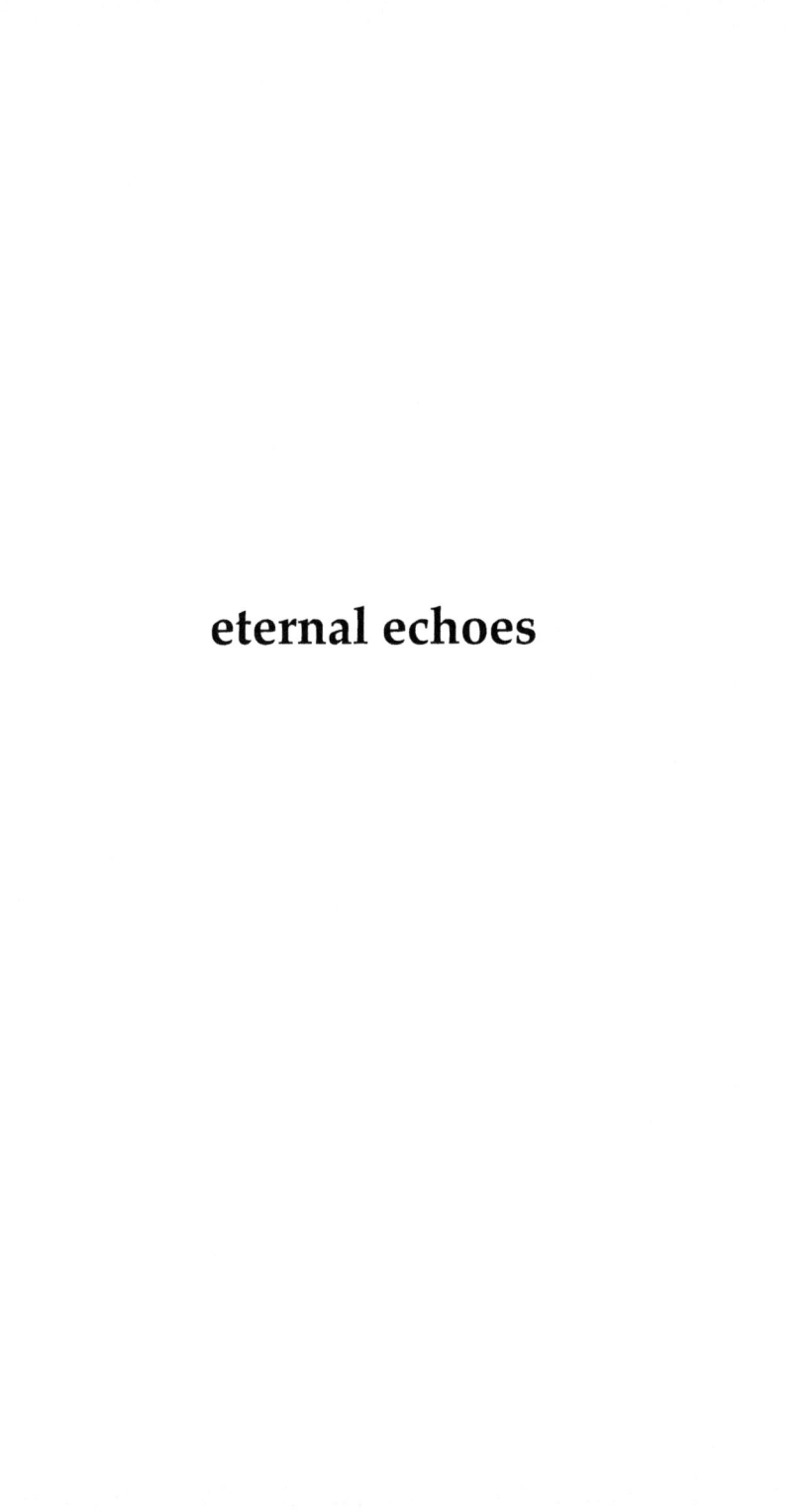

i remember your hand in mine
the warmth of your fingers
the curve of your palm
the smoothness of your skin

i remember your body next to mine
how it felt to be together
your laugh your smile
the smell of your hair

i remember the night you said you loved me
the night we first made love
i remember the warmth of your skin
as you lay next to me
and the softness of your hands
as they explored my body

i remember the sound of your voice
when you said my name
it echoed through me
like a distant memory
a sound i hadn't heard in years
yet one that still lingers on

the sweetest memories

are the ones

that never fade

that stay with us

keep us stronger

and happier

until the day we die

i remember

the taste of your lips
the smell of your skin
the feel of your hands
the sound of your laugh
the look in your eyes

like the echo of a memory
a long past whisper in the wind
into eternity

love leaves

lasting imprints

on our hearts

as they walk away

for a while

and when we think

that they have gone

they come back

to us again

echoes

like ripples at the surface

remain long after

we have disappeared

and went to the ground

returning to the womb

of mother earth

i am not the same
as i was
when you and i
were together

the world has changed
my body has changed
my skin no longer wears
your touch

but your scent remains
upon the pillow
where we once slept

eternal echoes of your voice
diminished by distance
in the absence of sight
in the absence of touch

your words remain
forever in my heart
like a poem
a scar

graved in gold
with love
like a song
in my mind

into dust

we take our love

and carry on

reaching for light and its shadows

every time i try to remember

how i lost you

how we broke apart

how we ended

my mind drifts into the memory

of the moment it all began

when we first met

i think of our story

like waves

at the surface of a lake

in the summer sun

the waves spread out

farther and farther

but soon disappears

we can see it for a moment

then it's gone

when the water has settled

you wonder

is anything left

i can't help but think

waves will be all that is left

of our story

the sound of your voice

takes the breath from my chest

ringing in my ears

like a sweet melody.

like a distant song

the whisper of a distant land

echoes of the heart

we cannot leave

our memories behind

even on the coldest night alone

the memory of love

lives on

the echo of love is like a river
that will never turn blue and cold
even in the depths of winter
it stays alive and flows through
our lives

it leaves no room for regrets
the river is your guide
it takes you where you have to go
as it washes you ashore in safety

don't try to go against the tide
for the current knows
where the pain of loneliness can be healed
by the love that awaits you

love is like a butterfly

going from one flower to the other

it can be found anywhere

but only for a moment

it never stays

as fragile as a wild rose

as colorful as a rainbow

after the rain

a new dawn breaks through

and dries the soaked ground

as the sun rises to shine on us again

the love we hold so dearly

is but an echo in our mind

longing for a presence

that will never return

so we yearn to live again

through memories

and hope that one day

we might again see a butterfly

about the author

luna osho is an aspiring poet who has chosen to be anonymous. she currently lives in a remote part of france with her beloved cat. she loves poetry, cinema, travel, and books. when she's not writing or reading, she enjoys watching films or visiting art museums. her dream is one day to become a full-time author while living and traveling all around the world. you can find out more about her on tiktok and instagram: @luna.osho

Printed in Great Britain
by Amazon